T0368212

The REVELATION

MINISTER MONTE MOORE

WESTBOW
PRESS®
A DIVISION OF THOMAS NELSON
& ZONDERVAN

WestBow Press books may be ordered through booksellers or by contacting:

WestBow Press
A Division of Thomas Nelson & Zondervan
1663 Liberty Drive
Bloomington, IN 47403
www.westbowpress.com
844-714-3454

Scriptures are taken from the Amplified Bible, Copyright © 2015 by The Lockman Foundation, La Habra, CA 90631. All rights reserved.

Scripture marked as (KJV) are taken from King James version of the Bible, public domain.

ISBN: 979-8-3850-0787-5 (sc)
ISBN: 979-8-3850-0788-2 (hc)
ISBN: 979-8-3850-0789-9 (e)

Library of Congress Control Number: 2023917718

Print information available on the last page.

WestBow Press rev. date: 11/20/2023

PREFACE

The Bible is constructed of 31,124 verses, and of these, 8,352 verses are prophetic. That means that 27 percent of the entire Bible is prophecy. The first prophecy is in Genesis 3:15, and it proclaims the coming of the Messiah; the last one is in Revelation 22:7, 20 and proclaims the coming of the Messiah: "surly I am coming quickly."

The first prophecy that mentions the second coming of Jesus is found in Jude 1:14 where Enoch prophesied saying, "Behold the Lord cometh with ten thousands of His holy ones." This prophecy was given before the flood. Yes, prophecy is a part of scripture. The reality of prophecy is that it is God speaking through humanity (2 Peter 1:19–21).

Prophecy proves the reliability of scripture (Isaiah 46:8–11). God says "I am God declaring the end from the beginning" for *His* purpose. It is not just people prophesying of their own free will, but God through individuals speaking to His people. Prophecy also gives us a better understanding of our time period (2 Timothy 3:1–5). As we look at this scripture, we see that the things that Timothy speaks of are some of the things that are happening right now. People today are lovers of themselves, lovers of money, boastful, disobedient, and unholy. In verse 1, we read "In the last days." This is in reference to when the Holy Spirit was poured out as described in the book of Acts (Acts 2:16–20).

The prophet Joel prophesied that God will pour out His Spirit on all humankind. Jesus told the disciples to stay in Jerusalem until the Holy Spirit arrived. When the Holy Spirit came upon them, the last days began. They will end with the return of the Lord. We are living in the last days. The last days could be a million years, from now; we do not know. Only God knows.

Note: Enoch was written about in Genesis 5:18–24; however, the book of Enoch was excluded from the Bible. I wonder why.

Prophecy gives comfort in sorrow (1 Thessalonians 4:13–18). The people believed that Jesus would return, but their major concern was what happens to the Christians who died before His return. Then Paul told them that the dead in Christ would rise first, so they didn't have to worry about their loved ones; they would participate in His coming (1 Corinthians 15:22–23).

The resurrection of Jesus Christ is proof of our resurrection. Their assurance was that those who had died would return with Christ. Prophecy proves that God is in control (Acts 4:25–29). Verse 27 shows that God appointed Herod, Pontius Pilate, the Gentiles, and the people of Israel to fulfill His purpose. Even the things that are happening around us today are still in God's control; they are happening for His glory. These things happen to fulfill His plan. Things do not just happen; they happen for a reason. Prophecy gives spiritual stability so that we should not be quickly shaken or disturbed when we hear that the day of the Lord has come. The people of the church of Thessalonica thought they had missed the coming of the Lord. They thought the Rapture had already taken place because of the persecution they were under. Paul had to show them that they had not missed the Rapture. He explained to them that the other things that had been prophesied had to happen first. In 2 Thessalonians 2:3–4, Paul reminded them that the man of lawlessness—the Antichrist—has to be revealed before the day of the Lord will come; this is prophesied in Daniel 9:26. The prince who is to come is the little horn in Daniel 7:8. As we look at prophecy from where we are today, we can take comfort in the things spoken to us by the prophets of the Old Testament concerning the coming of Jesus Christ. Looking to the future with what Jesus has said must come to past before His return.

INTRODUCTION

The book of Revelation begins with Jesus telling us that God gave Him a revelation to give to us. He wants us to know what is happening in the church today. God wants us to know what will happen to the church, the earth, and the people of this world in the future as well. The meaning is in the title of the book: "Revelation of Jesus Christ."

Revelation:

(1) *a surprising and previously unknown fact, especially one that is made known in a dramatic way*

(2) *the divine or supernatural disclosure to humans of something relating to human existence or the world*

(1) (2) dictionary.com

For the creation of the book of Revelation of Jesus Christ, God told Jesus what would happen, Jesus told one of the angels, the angel told or showed John, and John wrote it down for us to read.

The entire book of Revelation is outlined in chapter 1 verse 19:

Verse 19a: Write the things you have seen: what John saw in heaven (chapter 1).

Verse 19b: Write the things that are: what is happening in the church today (chapters 2–3).

Verse 19c: Write the things that will take place after these things, meaning what will happen in the future (chapter 4–22).

The Apostle John wrote the book of Revelation. He was the last living apostle; he had been exiled or sent to a small island in the Aegean Sea called Patmos. John was sent there by the Roman government to keep him from preaching and teaching about Jesus. John also wrote four other books in the Bible: the book of John and the first, second, and third books of John. Most of the information in the first twenty chapters of the book of Revelations can be found in the Old Testament. Some of the things revealed in the book of Revelation are spoken of in the New Testament, but not revealed. The last two chapters of the book are all about new events that will happen in the future. The book of Revelations takes Old Testament prophecies and puts them in order. The order of the events in some cases is not one right after the other; some events that are written of in later chapters of the book happen at the same time that events described in the first half of the book take place. The exact meaning of this prophecy may never be perfectly clear to us until it is fulfilled.

John's writing style is what we call apocalyptic; it is highly symbolic with pictorial representations such as beasts, dragons, and a dissolving universe. Some of the books of the Bible that we can use to understand the book of Revelations are Exodus, Psalms, Ezekiel, Daniel, Isaiah, and Zechariah.

ONE

Write the things that you see.
—Revelation 1:19

The first chapter of Revelation tells us what will be revealed and who is giving John this information: the Alpha and Omega, the first and the last, the beginning and the end (Revelation 1:8, 10).

The first chapter also tells us whom the book is written to. Keep in mind that the seven churches include the churches of today. John was in a trance, a daydream as some would say, but John was in the spirit on the Lord's Day (Revelation 1:10).

We live in two realms at the same time: the spiritual realm and the physical, three-dimensional realm. You believe in God, you believe He is alive, but you cannot see Him because He exists in the spiritual realm. We as human beings live in the physical realm, but we worship God in spirit (John 4:23–24).

The Lord's Day is the day God showed John the vision with no specific day, date, or time. John heard a voice that told him to write down what he saw in a book and send it to the seven churches: Ephesus, Smyrna, Pergamos, Thyatira, Sardis, Philadelphia, and Laodicea.

There were more than seven churches. These churches were in cities that could be compared to today's postal zones or zip codes where information and instruction from the emperor was given to the public.

The number seven represents completeness; this means that all churches were included.

John saw seven golden lampstands. Each lampstand represented one of the seven churches (Revelation 1:20).

John saw a man (the Son of Man) in a robe with a golden sash across His chest.

- Son of Man: Jesus
- Robe: garment of the high priest
- Golden sash: worn by the high priest when serving in the temple

So, the picture here is that Jesus was serving in His priestly duties. His head and hair were white like snow, His eyes were on fire, His feet were bronze, and He had a voice of many waters. In His right hand He had seven stars. A two-edged sword came out of His mouth, and His face was shining bright.

- White: glowing white represents His holiness
- Eyes burning like lasers, seeing into your heart: He sees through the fake stuff
- Bronze feet: divine judgment is coming
- Voice of many waters: authority
- Right hand: place of honor and power
- Seven stars: leaders and preachers of the seven churches (Revelation 1:20); also represents all leaders of the church today

MINISTER MONTE MOORE

- Two-edged sword: the word of God, used to judge, cuts both ways; an offensive and defensive weapon (Hebrews 4:12)
- Shining bright: you cannot hide; everything is revealed about you

John fell at His feet because he recognized who was talking to him. The last time John saw Jesus was when He was ascending into heaven (Acts 1:9–11).

I was alive, I was dead, now I live forever more, I have the keys to death and hell (Revelation 1:18).

- Alive: when Jesus was ministering
- Dead: when Jesus was crucified
- Alive forever: eternal life
- Keys: to control the opening and closing of doors
- Death: where our physical bodies go
- Hell: where the unsaved go

So chapter 1 of Revelation is about John looking into heaven and telling us where he was, what he saw, and who was talking to him.

TWO

Write the things that are.
—Revelation 1:19

Remember that, in chapter 1 of Revelation, John was told to write letters to the seven churches: Ephesus, Smyrna, Pergamos, Thyatira, Sardis, Philadelphia, and Laodicea. These churches represented the churches at that time and represent the churches today as well.

There are a couple of ways to look at these letters. First, the conditions described for each church that actually existed during the time that John wrote these letters. Second, these conditions are also a description of the church at any time in history, including today. Everything that is in the letters had happened or has been happening since the day of Pentecost (Acts 2). Third, the letters are a consecutive view of the history of the church. That means these letters match a given time period; we do not get to pick and choose which description fits the church that we attend. The fourth theory of the churches is that each description of the church is a representation of *our own personal* relationship with God.

Now let's look at the first letter. In verse 2, it says that this church left its first love. The loveless church of Ephesus was established in the first century AD 52; Jesus had been crucified, and the Romans were persecuting Christians. The church had lost its passion for Jesus. They were like a candle going out. The motive for their worship was missing, and that was Jesus, their first love.

Verse 6 says that the Ephesian church hated the Nicolaitans, a professional priesthood (priests for hire). They were evil. They called themselves messengers of God but were found to be impostors and liars. *Nicolaos* in the Greek language is broken down like this: *Nico* means "priest" and *Laos* means "people." The Nicolaitans were priests of the people. They were hired by the people to lead the church. They were men who went to God for the people.

Before Jesus died, a priest was the only person who could go to God for the people. After Jesus died, the curtain in the temple that separated the people from God was destroyed. Now we can go to God ourselves (Matthew 27:51; Mark 15:38; Luke 23:45).

The church at Smyrna was persecuted. This church was established at the end of the first century and lasted until the fourth century. This is where we see many depictions of Christians being used in the arenas of Rome. They were also run through with poles that were then put into the ground upright. At night the Christians would be burned and used as streetlights. This was during the time of Emperor Nero.

THREE

Write the things that are.
—Revelation 1:19

The church at Pergamos was the compromising church. It was established at the end of the fourth century and beginning of the fifth century. This church was controlled by the government; Christianity had become the religion of Rome. Constantine the Great, a Roman emperor, was the first to convert to Christianity. His mother was a Greek Christian, and his father was Flavius Constantius. Constantine had heard of Christianity from his mother, but what convinced him to become a Christian? He had heard the Christians who were being killed singing and praising God. Before going into battle with Maxentius, another Roman leader, he prayed for a sign from God that he would win the war. In his dream, he saw a cross. He felt it was a sign from God. He won the battle, converted to Christianity, and then declared Christianity the religion of Rome, meant to replace a mixture of pagan worship and philosophy with watered-down religious doctrine. In verse 13, Jesus calls this church the seat of Satan.

The church at Thyatira was a corrupt church. From the sixth century to the fifteenth century, this was the beginning of Catholicism, continuing the church under Roman rule and moving more toward pagan and idol worship in the church.

And now, as we move to chapter 3, we begin with the church of Sardis, the dead church. This church began in the sixteenth century and lasted through the seventeenth century. This church was known as a Christian church, but there was no spiritual life involving Jesus Christ. They just showed up and went through the motion of worshipping God.

The church at Philadelphia was a faithful church established during the first century. This is the church everyone wants to claim as their church in the twenty-first century, but this church has passed according to time. On a personal level, every Christian should strive to be this church that God loved because of the love it showed to Him.

The church at Laodicea was the lukewarm church. This is the church of today, and it will last until Jesus returns. This church is called the compromising, materialistic church. If you look around you today, that is exactly what you see in the church: pagan worship and idolatry. We have compromised our worship for the acceptance of the world. You cannot tell the difference between the activities of the church and the activities of the world. For example, the world celebrates Hallowe'en or All Hallows' Eve as it was called in the past. It is a high holiday for Wiccans, the religion of witchcraft. Many churches today have changed the name to Hallowed Night. It is celebrated at the same time as Hallowe'en.

Just because you change the name does not mean you change the reason for the celebration; this is compromise. The church of today practices some of the same pagan rituals that the Babylonians practiced in the past. We have taken the power out of the word of God to make it more pleasing to the world.

FOUR

Write the things that will be.
—Revelation 1:19

Chapter 4 of Revelation is thought to explain how the saved, or what we call born-again believers, will be taken into heaven. This is better known as the Rapture or the beginning of the Great Tribulation. Notice I did not say that God takes *Christians* to heaven, because not everyone who calls himself or herself a Christian is born again or recognized by God (Matthew 7:21–23; Luke 6:44–49; James 1:22–27).

One reason for the idea that this is the beginning of the Rapture is that John was asked to "come up" to heaven in verse 1, and this is supposed to represent the church going to heaven. Second, the church is never mentioned again as being on the earth after this incident, so it is assumed that the church, saints, believers, and all those who are born again have gone to heaven. The first time the church is mentioned is in Matthew 16:16–18, which says, "Upon this rock I will build my church." Yes, Peter is the beginning of the church. The beginning of the church in the spiritual realm is what Peter said: "You are the Christ, the Son of God." This is the philosophy the church is built on.

Anyone who believes that Jesus is the Son of God believes that Jesus is the church, not the building. "I will build *My church*" means that the church belongs to the Lord. God revealed to Peter that Jesus was His son. The church isn't something that is formed by a human organization.

"The church" is used nineteen times in chapters 1 through 3 and is not used at all in chapters 5 through 21. Then, in chapter 22, the church, or bride, is used four times. This is another reason I think we are in heaven (Revelation 21:2, 9; 22:16–17).

Another point I would like to make is that Jesus said we, the church, would sit on thrones and judge with Him (1 Corinthians 6:2–3; Revelation 3:21). The picture that John gives us is that the elders are seated on thrones around God's throne. There are smaller thrones around the elders where we, as the church, will sit and judge with Jesus (1 Corinthians 6:2–3).

So, if the church is not in heaven and is not mentioned again as the church on *earth*, then my question to you is where is it? Once the church has left the earth, God can now deal with the unbelieving Jews and Gentiles for their rejection of the Messiah, Jesus Christ. This time period is called the Great Tribulation, seven year's dedicated to the judgement of humanity. In the beginning of chapter 4 we see that John is asked to go come up to heaven. Once John got into heaven, he saw a throne, and the one sitting on the throne was shining brightly like precious stones with the light of the sun shining through Him. Around the throne, there were twenty-four smaller thrones with twenty-four people sitting on them. The people sitting on the smaller thrones were called elders; they were dressed in white, and they had crowns on their heads. There is no specific information on who these elders are.

- Sitting on thrones: they are ready to judge (1 Corinthians 6:2–3)
- Elders: these represent the church as a whole (Revelation 3:21; 1 Corinthians 6:2–3)

- Dressed in white: overcomer's (Revelation 3:5; Revelation 19:7–8)
- Crowns: Not crowns of royalty, but reward or victory crowns, a wreath crown, like the ones you see the Roman Olympians receiving after a victory

The elders were wearing crowns because they had already been given their rewards; they were sitting on their thrones ready to judge (Daniel 7:9–10).

In front of the throne were seven lamps of fire that represent the seven-fold Spirit of God—the fullness or *complete spirit of God*, the *Holy Spirit* (Isaiah 11:2).

Seven is the number of completeness: Spirit of God, understanding, counsel, wisdom, power, Knowledge, Fear of God.

Those of the Jewish faith recognize the seven-fold Spirit of God in the symbol of the Menorah (Zechariah 4:2).

Around the throne of God there were four living creatures called angels. There are four different groups of angels with many different ranks. The first living creature is like a lion, the second is like a calf, the third is like the face of a man, and the fourth is like a flying eagle.

- Lion: represents Jesus's kingship
- Calf or bullock: represents His sacrifice as a servant
- Face of a man: a symbol of His humanity: The Son of Man
- Eagle: a symbol of His deity as creator, supreme being, the Son of God
- Wings: for swiftness in serving God.

These angels had eyes all over themselves, which represents that they could see and understand all things. Their job was to worship God and never stop. They engaged in ceaseless worship of God (Isaiah 6:2–3).

This vision prepares us for what is to follow, God is seen as the almighty ruler of the universe sitting on the throne of His glory, surrounded by worshiping creatures, and about to pronounce judgment on the earth.

These creatures are created beings, because they worship God, they seem to be a combination of the cherubim (burning judgment) in Ezekiel 10 and the seraphim (burning purification) in Isaiah 6, they are the guardians of the throne of God.[1]

---

[1]   William Macdonald, *Believers Bible Commentary* (Nashville TN: Thomas Nelson Publishing, 1995) 2468–2469.

FIVE

In chapter 5 of Revelation, we see that John was still in the throne room of heaven, and God had a book or scroll in His hand with seven wax seals keeping it closed. The scroll contains the first seven judgements that humanity and the earth must go through. Each seal represent's a different judgement, and the seventh seal is not only a judgement in itself, but it is also the beginning of the first trumpet judgement.

Books like we have today did not exist then. Scrolls were rolled up, and made of papyrus, a material made from the stems of a water plant that are crushed, pressed together, and then dried. Scrolls were used to write down information that was needed in contracts between two or more people such as deeds to property. Detailed information was written on the inside of the scroll, and a summary of this information was written on the outside. Wax seals were used to seal the contract to keep the agreement private; only the owner of the scroll had the authority to open it. This scroll is the deed of ownership of the earth (Luke 4:5–7).

- When Adam sinned, he gave Satan the deed or rights to rule the earth.

- The Scroll of Daniel (Daniel 12:4) was sealed until the end time.
- The Scroll of Redemption (Romans 8:20–24) is an agreement that all of creation is coming back to God.

The scroll that was in Gods hand was a combination of all three of these. In verse 2, an angel asked, "Who is worthy to open the scroll"? But it seemed that there was no one worthy to open it; only one who had authority or ownership of the scroll could open it. John began to cry because he knew that, if no one could open the scroll, creation could not be redeemed or given back to God. Then one of the elders told John to stop crying and to look. The Lion of the tribe of Judah had the authority to open the scroll. But when John looked, he saw a lamb that looked as if it had been killed, not a strong ferocious lion. This lamb had seven horns on its head, and it had seven eyes.

- The Lamb of God: Jesus
- The lamb looked dead but was alive: the death and resurrection of Jesus
- The lamb was standing: because He has not finished His assignment of redeeming humanity, he could not sit down yet
- Seven: completeness
- Horns: because he had seven horns, he has complete authority
- Eyes: omniscience, knowing everything completely

When the Lamb took the scroll, heaven rejoiced. They celebrated because what had been prophesied by the prophets was happening right in front of their eyes. Each elder had a harp and a golden bowl of incense. The harp was used as an instrument in praise and worship to God; it was also used as the prophets prophesied to the people (1 Samuel 10:5).

These golden wide mouth saucers/bowls were common in the tabernacle and temple. Priest stood two times a day in front of the inner veil of the temple and burned incense so that the smoke would go into the Holy of Holies and be swept into the nostrils of God, it was a symbol of the prayers of the people rising up to God.[2]

---

[2] *New American Standard Bible*, comments section verse 8 (Nashville TN: Thomas Nelson publishing, 2006) 1969.

SIX

In chapters 4 and 5 of Revelation, we read that all born-again believers have gone to heaven to be with Jesus. This event is called the Rapture, which, in simple terms, means "taken up." The word *rapture* is not a part of the original Hebrew language. It is translated from the Greek word *harpazo*, which means "to seize" or "to take away" and the Latin word *raptio*, which has the same meaning. This is where we get the word *rapture* from, meaning taken up or going to heaven without experiencing death. People in Old Testament times knew about the Rapture, but it was a mystery to them. This mystery has been revealed to us in the New Testament. Paul taught the Thessalonian and the Corinthian churches about the Rapture (1 Thessalonians 4:13–18; 1 Corinthians 15:50–58).

There will be no sign given letting us know when the Rapture will happen, and there will be no announcement of its coming. No one knows the day or the hour that this event will take place; we just know that it will take place. At the time of the Rapture, those who are *not* born again will be left here on earth to go through a time period called the Great Tribulation, which is broken into two parts. The first part (Revelation 6–9) will be approximately three and a half years long. The entire Tribulation is supposed to last seven years. It is also known as the seventieth week of Daniel (Daniel 9:24). I suggest that you read all of Chapter 9 in the book of Daniel.

Chapter 6 tells us what is happening on earth during this time period as Jesus breaks the seals one by one. The first seal will be broken, and a rider on a white horse will be released into the earth. The rider is presumed to be the Antichrist. Some churches teach that this rider is Jesus, but if you remember, in chapter 5, Jesus is portrayed as the slain Lamb in heaven. So this rider cannot be Jesus; He will return on a horse with a sword at the end of the Great Tribulation.

These riders represent evil spiritual forces or demons, not necessarily people as John described him. The spirit of this rider, as he is released into the earth, will enter a live person. This person will probably be a high-ranking government official who is recognized throughout the world.

The rider of the white horse will have a bow but no arrows; he will be given a crown, and God will give him the authority to go conquer on the earth.

- White horse: world peace. But it is a false sense of peace; the entire world will follow him to find this peace.
- Bow: a symbol of war. The lack of arrows means it is a bloodless war. This war will be won by the alliance and agreement of multiple nations that will join together for their own mutual benefits (think of it as NATO).
- Crown: a crown like the one given to athletes. It is a wreath crown, not a crown of royalty.
- Rider: the Antichrist (it is assumed that he is the rider). This is a real human being possessed by the spirit of the Antichrist.

Note: On August 13, 2020, Jarad kushner negotiated the Abraham Accords with Israel, the Unite Arab Emirates, Egypt, and Jordan. No, I do not think that this is the peace treaty referred to in the Bible because the Bible says the world will be at peace, and the world is not at peace. But, as you can see, things that are spoken of are beginning to happen.

This first rider will bring unity to all the nations, fix the world's economy, and make an agreement with Israel to keep the inhabitants safe and secure. But it will not last. The second seal will be opened, a red horse will be summoned, and this rider will be given a sword.

- Red horse: a symbol of war and bloodshed (Matthew 24:7–8)
- Sword: a short weapon for close-contact fighting, something like a dagger, quick and easy to maneuver (Daniel 8:24)

God will grant this rider the power to create worldwide war (1 Thessalonians 5:3). This is one of the many signs of the beginning of the birth pains. The beginning of the wrath of God is compared to the pain that a woman feels when she is about to give birth (Matthew 24:4–8; Mark 13:7–8; Luke 21:9–10).

The first rider brought a sense of peace and tranquility to the world, but it will be a false sense of peace. It will feel real, but it won't be. I'm sure all of the people will be having fun and feel that nothing could go wrong. Then, after the second seal is broken, the war and killing will begin. A deadly spiritual force will be released on humanity through the rider of the red horse, and people will begin slaying one another. This war will be started under the delusion of protecting themselves and their countries from others who might attack, but this will quickly turn into the killing of each other for the sport of it.

When the third seal is broken, a rider on a black horse will be released, and the rider will be holding a pair of balancing scales. "A quart of wheat and three quarts of barley for a denarius" said a voice that came from the midst of the living creatures. "Do not damage the wine and oil."

The black horse is a symbol of famine and a lack of essential items for life. Everything will be rationed and weighed with the scales of the rider of the black horse.

A denarius was a Roman coin. It's worth was approximately $32 in today's money, the amount a person might be paid for one day of work. A denarius could buy ten quarts of wheat and thirty quarts of barley in the days of the Roman Empire, enough to feed an entire family. However, during the time of the Tribulation, one denarius will buy only one quart of wheat, just enough for one person for one day.

Oil and wine could possibly have two meanings. These were luxury items obtainable in large quantities only by the rich people. For the poor, small amounts of oil were used to make bread, and wine was used for cooking, purifying water, and also as medicine.

After any war, there is always a lack of essential supplies that people need to survive. The land will be destroyed and the soil will be contaminated; crops will not grow. Banks, gas stations, and stores of all kinds will all be closed. Most of the merchandise will be looted or destroyed. There will be no Wi-Fi, no cell phones, no electricity. None of the things we take for granted today will exist.

When the fourth seal is broken, a pale horse and rider will be released. Unlike the other riders, this rider has a name, and his name is Death, and hades follows him. Death is what happens to the physical body when we die. Hades is where our spirits or souls go after death until the time of Judgement.

The fourth rider will have the authority to kill one-fourth of the world's population. Now, you must remember that there has already been a world war, and worldwide famine has followed. We do not know how many people survived the two previous events, but one-fourth of those survivors will be killed. Just to give you an idea of how many people that will be, there are approximately eight billion people on the planet today. So one-fourth of today's population would be two billion people. If we start on the eastern border of Texas and draw a line from the Gulf of Mexico all the way up to Canada, every man, woman, and child in all of the states west of that line represent those who will be killed. From the west coast of California to the eastern border of Texas, from the Gulf of Mexico to Canada, including Alaska and Hawaii, would equal two billion people. Some have wondered if there will be anyone saved after the Rapture, during the Great Tribulation. Chapter 20 will answer that question.

When the fifth seal is broken, the cries of the martyrs will be heard, and their souls will be seen underneath the altar in heaven. Here in the opening of the fifth seal we see those who have been killed during the opening of the first four seals.

Altar here probably refers to the altar where the incense is burned. The smoke of the incense represents the prayers of the saints going up to God.

These martyrs are the people who were killed because of their testimony of Jesus Christ during their time on the earth at the time of the Great Tribulation. They were crying out to God asking Him how long it would before He would avenge their deaths. God told them to rest a little while longer because there were others who must be martyred before He can avenge them. Then God will give each one of them a white robe as proof of their righteousness. He will answer their prayers, but He will decide when it is time. God has established predetermined times for all things. We must remember that there are no time limits in the spiritual realm where God lives. Our time limits are not Gods time limits.

All of the events I've mentioned here, from the opening of the first seal to the pouring out of the seventh bowl, will take place in approximately two and a half years. The exact time span between each sign is unknown, but it is believed that they happen one right after the other.

When the sixth seal is opened, there will be a worldwide earthquake. Every fault line in the world will move at the same time. This earthquake will cause mountains to crumble. Islands will disappear because of the rise of the water level, and continents will split apart. History tells us that the continents have broken apart before, so it is not that hard to believe that this could happen again.

The San Francisco earthquake of 1906 was a magnitude 7.9 on the Richter scale; the entire city was devastated. The earthquake ignited a fire that burned for four days and destroyed twenty-eight thousand buildings. All of the buildings in a five-hundred-city-block radius were completely leveled to the ground. That was one earthquake in one city. Now imagine the entire world shaking like the city of San Francisco, all at the same time. That will give you an idea of how intense this earthquake will be. The Bible says that the sun will become black as sackcloth. (Sackcloth is a piece of fabric that is made from goat hair. It is dense and difficult to see through.)

This is my assumption of why the sun will become black: The prediction does not mean that the sun will stop producing heat and light. If that were to happen, everything on the planet would die. Besides, later, in chapter 8, it say's that the sun will become dim, so the sun is not burning out as some would assume.

If everyone and everything on the planet were to die at the opening of the sixth seal, then the book of Revelation would end there. Humans are needed on the earth to fulfill the rest of the book of Revelation. The sun will appear to turn black because of the numerous volcano's erupting around the world that will spew gasses, steam, smoke, and ash into the atmosphere in such concentration as to block the light of the sun. Remember that John had never seen anything like this before in his entire life, so he was explaining to us what he was seeing in the only way he could understand it.

Today we have a better understanding of what these things will look like. We can explain them as we know them or have seen them.

John wrote that the moon will look like blood. I live in Southern California, and we have a lot of brush fires and forest fires that put a lot of smoke into the atmosphere. As the sun goes down, the rays of light going through the smoke turn the entire sky into an array of different colors—blue, purple, red, orange, and yellow. This same effect, I think, will make the moon appear red or like blood. The color will be caused by light shining through the smoke from the volcanos that are erupting. Now, once again, we have to remember that we are talking about volcanos erupting simultaneously all around the world.

We also, from time to time, observe a phenomenon called a blood moon. This happens when the moon is in a total eclipse and appears reddish in color. It is illuminated by sunlight filtered and refracted by the earth's atmosphere.

These are my suggestions of what will be happening, and I could very well be wrong in my assumptions, so, I will take this time to remind you to read and pray about what you read. Do not just accept anyone's opinion about it, even mine.

I interpret the stars falling from heaven as a meteor shower or something like that, which is very common today.

So, after all of the events that have occurred, the people who remain on the earth will finally realize that something catastrophic is happening. Fear will come upon them, but this will not be the normal type of fear that we know; it will be beyond the basic human emotion. I have been afraid before, but never with fear that can be compared to the fear I anticipate this to be. I can't imagine being so afraid that I would want a rock or mountain to fall on me just to keep me from coming into the presence of God. This type of fear is beyond understanding for a normal person, and a fear I do not want to know.

SEVEN

At the end of chapter 6 of Revelation, we read that the people finally realize that something out of the ordinary has been happening to them. The unbelievers recognize that what has been happening is the wrath of God. They will ask the rocks to fall on them so that they will not have to face God. They will want to hide themselves from His presence. The one question that stands out at the end of chapter 6 is who is able to stand? The answer is no one. God's wrath will be so severe that no one believes that he or she can survive what has been happening.

But, throughout history, God has always shown us mercy and grace. He has always been willing to forgive us, reclaim us to Himself, and still call us His sons and daughters. Chapter 7 is proof of that willingness to forgive people even during His time of wrath on an unsaved world. In Revelation 7:1, John wrote about seeing four angels holding back the wind from the four corners of the earth. No wind was blowing, not even a whisper of a breeze. Judgement had been stopped for a time. Then God will send another angel to tell the four angels holding back the wind to not harm the earth until He can seal his servants on their foreheads. This seal on the forehead of

His servants indicates that He owns them and no one else can harm them. It is like the seals on the scroll that we read about Jesus opening in chapter 6. As we discussed earlier, this stamp or seal is proof of ownership. God is saying these belong to Him. No one is to mess with them. The seal contained two names which were printed on the forehead of these chosen ones; God and Jesus were those names (Revelation 14:1).

The Antichrist will also require a mark or the sign 666 for his followers. He has always tried to be like God; that is why he was kicked out of heaven: he wanted to be God. The number of servants who will receive the seal will be 144,000. They will be chosen to serve as God's ministers. This represents 12,000 people from each tribe of Israel. Some religions teach that this is the number of people who will make it into heaven, but that is not true. The Bible is specific in saying "from every tribe of Israel." Now let's take a look in the book of Genesis. This is where God changed Jacob's name to Israel, and his twelve sons generated the twelve tribes of Israel (Genesis 32:28). The twelve tribes were Reuben, Simeon, Judah, Naphtali, Gad, Asher, Issachar, Zebulun, Benjamin, Joseph, Manasseh, and Levi. There were two tribes left out, and one was renamed—the tribe of Dan. Some think that this is the tribe that the Antichrist will come from (Genesis 49:17).

The tribe of Ephraim was also left out. These two tribes were the leaders of idolatry and sorcery within the nation of Israel. Ephraim was the son of Joseph, so the name of the tribe was changed to Joseph. Also included in this list was the tribe of Levi, the priestly tribe, who did not receive land at the time they entered the Promised Land.

The 144,000 will be witnesses for God on earth during the Great Tribulation. Their number-one mission will be to tell everyone that there is still time left to repent of their evil ways and return to the Lord. Gods grace and mercy will still be at work even during the time of His wrath. Some of those who will be left behind after the Rapture will become born-again believers. People from every nation, speaking different languages, will all stand before the throne in white robes waving palm branches. Their white robes will represent their righteousness. Palm branches were traditionally used in celebrations in ancient times. They will be used to celebrate being with the Lord. You would too if you had to go through what they went through or see what they have seen.

Joseph's two sons born in Egypt were adopted by Jacob. Their names were Ephraim and Manasseh. The name of the tribe of Ephraim was changed to Joseph because of their pagan worship. The tribe of Daniel is also suggested in some studies to have been involved in pagan worship, but the Bible is not specific, so I cannot be specific; this is just for information only.

EIGHT

The church age has ended, and all of the believers in Christ have gone to heaven. This is also known as the beginning of Daniel's seventieth week, which will last approximately seven years. Daniel's seventieth week, or the Great Tribulation, will be a time of God's judgement of humanity and the earth. As we begin chapter 8, we will be at a point in time of approximately eighteen to twenty-two months into this seven-year period. We will have a false sense of peace and hope. We have experienced a world war, worldwide famine, and a worldwide earthquake. When the church age ended and the Great Tribulation began, it seemed that all of these other things also began at approximately the same time.

Chapter 4 and 5: All believers go to heaven.

Chapter 6: The seven seals are opened.

Chapter 7: The 144,000 Jews chosen by God.

Chapter 8: The first four trumpets are blown.

Chapter 9: The last three trumpets are blown.

Chapter 17: The Babylonian religious system ends.

Chapter 18: The Babylonian political/economical system ends.

Chapters 17 and 18 describe one world religion, one world financial system, and one world political system. Think of it as a type of United Nations that we have today. By the end of chapter 8, today's financial and political systems have failed, or are in the process of completely failing.

Now, as the seventh seal is broken, seven trumpets, or shofar, will be revealed. A shofar was a large ram's horn blown like a trumpet. It was used in ancient Jewish religious ceremonies to call the people to the temple; and at the end of a festival. The shofar was also used as a battle signal.

Remember that, in chapter 7, God gave those who were left behind one more chance to repent when He held back the wind from the four corners of the earth.

There was silence in heaven. Why silence? The Bible doesn't explain it, so I will not attempt to. Let's leave it at that. When the seventh seal is opened, there will be no specific judgement connected to this seal. The seventh seal will open the seven trumpets. There will be seven angel's standing in front of God, and each one will be given a trumpet. The first four trumpets affect people's environment, and the last three trumpets will directly affect people themselves.

An eighth angel, whom most scholars identify as Jesus, will appear holding a golden censer. He will be given incense to burn in it. This time, Jesus will not be portrayed as a lamb; here we will see Him at His priestly duties, presenting our prayers to the Father. In the tabernacle and the temple, the priest would take the golden censer with burning incense into the Holy place. The smoke rising from the incense represented the prayers of the people rising up to God. In this illustration, Jesus will have the prayers of the martyrs that are under the alter, and He will throw them down to the earth. When Jesus throws the incense down, it will cause thunder, lighting, and earthquakes.

A golden censer is a pan suspended on a rope or chain. It was used to transport fiery coals from the brazen altar to the altar of incense in the tabernacle. Coals from the brazen altar were put into the pan to light the incense. The smoke rising up out of the pan was a symbol of the prayers of the people going up to God.

The prayers of the saints will return to the earth in wrath as the seven trumpet judgments are introduced with a violent disturbance of nature. When the first trumpet is sounded, there will be hail and fire mixed with blood that will fall to the earth. One-third of the trees on the earth and all of the grass will be consumed by the fire; one-third of the entire earth will be burned. This destruction is mainly in areas where food supplies are grown. Food will already be scarce after the world war, so even that supply of food will drastically be diminished. When the second angel blows his trumpet, something the size of a big mountain on fire will be thrown into the sea, and part of sea will become blood. We can most likely interpret this big rock or mountain as a meteorite. Scientists say this has already happened many times before and is still occurring today. The latest incident occurred in 2013 somewhere in Russia. The remnants of the largest impact on earth are in south Africa, and it is a crater ninety-nine miles wide.

One-third of all the sea creatures will be killed, and one-third of the world's ships will be destroyed—not just war ships, but ships used to move food and supplies around the world. So now we have volcanoes erupting and the trees and grass burning. The air quality will be terrible. Now imagine what the smell will be like with all of the dead sea creatures that wash up on the beaches. With a world war, worldwide famine, and worldwide earthquakes, the earth is not going to be a place you will want to live during this time. The one thing we should take away from this is that, if we do not make the first trip, God will be accepting reservations for the second trip (Revelation 7:14).

When the third trumpet is blown, a star will fall from heaven burning like a torch. It will fall on one-third of the fresh water in the world. This star has a name: Wormwood, which means bitter or poisonous. In Revelation 1:20, we see that the word star is used to describe an angel.

Usually when a word is used to describe a symbol, it is normally used to represent that same symbol throughout the book. So, we take that meaning to be the same thing here. John was describing an angel. He described this star as falling from heaven burning *like* a torch. This could possibly have been a fallen angel who was aligned with Satan.

When the fourth trumpet sounds, one-third of the sun, moon, and the stars will lose their illumination. They will become dim like a flashlight with weak batteries—the light will still come on, but it can hardly be used to find anything in the dark. With one-third of the sun gone, what will the temperature be like on earth? With the sun, moon, and the stars damaged, they will not be able to produce light.

When we study the Bible, it is good to remember that there are a lot of things that will not be explained completely until they happen. In Exodus 10:21, we see the use of the word *star* again, but this time it is not referring to a fallen angel. This is because it is mentioned specifically with a celestial body. First, it is not described as falling. Second, it is described with the sun and the moon. The way it is used with this fourth trumpet of judgement actually refers to the stars you see at night when you look up into the sky.

After this, John heard a voice, looked up, and saw an eagle flying around overhead saying, "Woe, woe, woe." In some Bible translations, the eagle is a representation of an angel. In chapter 4, one of the angels around the throne of God had the head of an eagle, so this could possibly be him.

These three woes are a warning to the people on earth of what is about to happen when the last three trumpets sound. These last three trumpets will herald disasters worse than the first seven seals and the first four trumpets. The first four trumpets have affected the environment; now the last three trumpets will directly impact humanity.

Let's review what has happened to the earth, man, sun, moon, stars, and water up to this point.

Earth

1. World war (6:4)
2. Famine (6:5)
3. Earthquake (6:13)
4. Meteor shower (6:13
5. Hail (8:7)
6. Fire (8:7)
7. Mountains falling (6:14)
8. Islands disappearing (6:14)
9. Everything burned (8:7)

Humanity

1. False peace (6:2)
2. World war (6:4)
3. Famine (6:8)
4. Pestilence (6:8)
5. Wild beast (6:8)
6. Poisoned (8:11)
7. One-quarter killed (6:8)
8. Salvation (6:8)

Sun

1. Becomes black (6:12)
2. One-third dies, goes out (8:12)

Moon

1. Looks like blood (6:12)
2. One-third dies, goes out (8:12)

Stars

1. Fall (6:12)
2. One-third dies, goes out (8:12)

Sky

Rolls up (6:14)

Seas and Oceans

1. Burning mountain falls in (8:8)
2. One-third becomes blood (8:8)
3. One-third poisoned (8:11)
4. One-third of sea creatures die (8:8)

Trees and Grass

One-third burned (8:7)

NINE

As we leave chapter 8 of Revelation with the eagle flying in what is left of the sky, he is crying "Woe, woe, woe" because of what is about to happen—one woe for each of the next three trumpets.

When the fifth angel blows his trumpet, an angel will fall from the sky to the earth. He will have the keys to the Abyss, the bottomless pit, a temporary holding place for fallen angels, demons, and spirits (Luke 8:30–31). The name of this fallen angel is Abaddon (Hebrew), which means destruction, or Apollyon (Greek), which means destroyer. Some resources say that this is Satan himself because he is the leader of this group.

As he opens the gates to the Abyss, smoke will come pouring out and cover the sky. Out of the smoke will emerge locust-like creatures. These are not like the locust we know of today, which are small insects; these creatures that John saw were like horses ready for battle. They will have crowns made of gold on their heads, and they will have the faces of humans. They will also have hair like a woman's, teeth like a lion's, breastplates to protect their vital organs, wings to fly with, and tails like those of scorpions. John compared them to locusts because of their ability to swarm together; he had seen the swarming ability of the insect and related that swarming ability with these creatures.

- Horse ready for battle: represents a conquering host
- Gold crown: they were authorized to rule
- Human face: sign of intelligence
- Hair like a woman's: attractive and seductive
- Teeth like a lion's: they were ferocious and cruel
- Breastplate: difficult to attack and destroy
- Scorpion tails: to torture people mentally and physically

These creatures have been told that they cannot harm the vegetation. Their assignment is to torment humankind, but they will not have the authority to kill. They may torment humankind for five months, which is how long the insect we know of today actually lives.

The only people they will not be able to harm are those who wear the seal of God on their foreheads (Revelation 7). The symptoms of this torment are the same as actually being stung by a scorpion: sweating, pale skin, fast breathing, fast heartbeat, high blood pressure, uncontrolled foamy saliva, wheezing, blurred vision, and more.

With a normal scorpion sting there is a possibility of death, but with these creatures, death will have been withheld by God. That means that, even when people try to commit suicide to avoid the torment, they will not die.

When the sixth trumpet sounds, a voice from the four horns of the golden altar that is in front of God will tell the angel with the trumpet to release the four angels that are bound in the River Euphrates.

Because the voice comes from the golden altar that is in front of God, some teachers connect this trumpet with the request of vengeance from the saints under the altar as well (Revelation 6:9–10).

In chapter 8, we also read that Jesus threw hot coals and incense to the earth. That was also supposed to be a part of the revenge of the martyrs. Now these four fallen angels will be released to kill one-third of the world's population. An army of two hundred million horsemen will be ready for battle. But the riders will not be the threat; it will be the horse that will do the killing. They will be wearing breastplates that are colored red, blue, and yellow. They will have the head of a lion; they will breathe fire, smoke, and sulfur; and they will have tails like those of scorpions. That their power is in their mouths may indicate that this description is of someone who is an eloquent speaker.[3] But behind the delusion will be the power of Satan, or demon spirit of Satan.

- Sulfur, smoke, fire: plagues, sickness, and disease
- Serpent/scorpion tail: used to wound and inflict pain

This eloquent speaker will be able to make people believe anything they might say, something like a politician: on the campaign trail, he will promise you anything if you vote for him, but once he is elected, you will never see any of the things that were promised. Even after all that has happened, the people will not repent; they will continue to believe and trust in their idols made of gold, silver, wood, and stone.

Note: As we see the description of the animals, stars, etc., we must remember that John saw these things in the spiritual realm. As they present themselves on earth, they will be in the form of human beings inhabited by demons or evil spirits. As an example, think of movie *The Exorcist* or stories about a zombie apocalypse. My point is for you to visualize what will be happening and understand how these things will manifest themselves.

---

[3]   Hamilton Smith, *The Revelation: An Expository Outline*. () 57.

TEN

The next five chapters of the book of Revelation—10 through 15—describe what will happen in what we think is the middle of the Great Tribulation. The events in all of these chapters will be happening simultaneously. The events in chapters 17 and 18 have also begun. These two chapters begin around the end of the events in chapter 4 and the beginning of chapter 5. At this point in the beginning of chapter 10, we read that the judging has stopped, but only for a moment. Just because the judging has stopped does not mean that there is peace on the earth.

1. The seven seal judgments have been opened.
2. 144,000 Jews have been chosen (chapter 7).
3. Great multitudes of people have been saved, through the ministry of the 144,000.
4. The fourth trumpet containing three woes, one for each of the remaining trumpets (chapter 9) has been blown.

The world will be in a state of devastation, and this brief period of silence will be much needed for those who are left on the earth to reflect and think about what has happened to them. But they still will not repent. At the beginning of chapter 10, John wrote about seeing another strong angel come down from heaven. Many think that this is Jesus because he has a rainbow on his head. The rainbow is a reminder of God's covenant to Noah. His face is shining, which represents God's glory. His feet are like pillars of fire, representing strength. Fire also represents judgment. The angel will put one foot on the land and one foot on the sea, which is a sign of his authority. This angel will hold a book in his hand; Jesus also held a book in his hand. The book that Jesus was holding was the title deed to the earth; the book that this angel will hold will be a record of the coming judgments.

When the angel spoke, John was ready to write what he said because, in chapter 1, he had been told to write the things that he heard and saw, but not this time.

The Bible doesn't say who this is, but if you study your Bible, you learn that, when Jesus returns, He will return ready to go to war with the Antichrist. Jesus will also be riding a white horse and carrying a two-edged sword. So, in my opinion, this is not Jesus. John wrote that he saw *another* angel. The Greek word for "another" is *allos,* and it is translated as "another of the same kind." There are many angels and ranks of angels but only one Jesus. There cannot be another one of the same kind if we are speaking of Jesus because there is only one Jesus.

The book will contain a heavenly message from the Lord from heaven to the earth. The angel will lift his hand toward heaven and make an oath to God. The oath that the angel proclaims will be that, when the seventh angel blows his trumpet, the bowl judgments will begin. Once this horn is blown and the six bowl judgments are poured out, one right after the other, the *mystery* of God will be finished and the Millennial Kingdom will be established. The mystery of God consists of spiritual truths revealed by God through divine inspiration. These truths were never previously known; they are truths that human intellect could never discover. (See Matthew 13:11, 35; Romans 16:25–26; Ephesians 3:4–5,9; and Colossians 1:26.)

What mystery of God will be finished?

1. The Great Tribulation
2. The second coming of the Messiah
3. Resurrection of the Old Testament saints
4. Resurrection of the tribulation believers
5. Establishing the Millennial Kingdom
6. Satan being chained and cast into the abyss for one thousand years

All of these things were written about in the Old Testament and revealed in the New Testament. John was told to take the book from the angel and eat it—not physically eat it, but read it, understand it, and then teach others what is in the book. The book would be sweet to the taste, but it would make one's stomach bitter or upset. The sweetness of what is in the book is Gods glory and our victory through him. The bitterness is seeing Gods wrath poured out on the ones that rejected His Son. After John ate (understood) the book, he was told that he was to go tell everyone about the bitter judgement of the seventh trumpet that reveals the seven bowls.

ELEVEN

John was given a rod with which to measure the temple and the altar. Then he was to count the people who were there worshiping. The temple being measured was the one in Jerusalem during the time of the Great Tribulation. In some teachings, it is called the tribulation temple. There has not been a temple on the Temple Mount since the one that was destroyed two thousand years ago. The part of the temple that John was to measure was the holy place and the holiest of holies, not the entire complex. The people would once again begin to worship God and make sacrifices in the temple. When the Antichrist declares himself to be god, he will desecrate the temple and the sacrifices will stop once again. Measuring the temple is a symbol of Gods ownership. The worshipers from the Tribulation will approach God via the altar. This is proof that some who go through the Tribulation will be saved.

John was told *not* to measure the outer court where the Gentiles were allowed to worship; they were not allowed in the inner court. This is nothing new; the Gentiles were never allowed in the inner court of the temple. Even when Jesus was ministering, they were not allowed in this area because they were considered to be unclean.

John not measuring the outer court is a sign of Gods rejection of the unbelieving Gentiles.

There will be two witnesses appointed to minister to the people. They will have supernatural powers, and their authority will be given to them by God. They will be instructed to preach a message of judgment and salvation during the second half of the Great Tribulation.

This is all a part of the God's testimony to Israel and the offer of salvation for their repentance. These two witnesses are also described as olive trees and lamp-stands (Zechariah 4:11–14).

- Olive tree: The oil in the fruit represents being filled with the Holy Spirit. The olive oil is also used to light the lamp-stands
- Lamp-stand: These bring light to darkness and also represent spiritual revival.

The olive tree's connection to the lamp-stands is an endless supply of oil to keep the light burning; this is a sign of their connection to the Holy Spirit of God. These two witnesses are thought to be Moses and Elijah. Some sources lean toward Jeremiah as being one as well. Other views include Enoch and Elijah because they never died physical deaths.

The book of Malachi specifically speaks of Elijah as being one of the witnesses (Malachi 4:5). They will have supernatural powers. They will be invincible and cannot be killed, but they can only use their power to protect themselves. These are some of the miraculous things they will be able to do.

- Fire will come from their mouths—Elijah (2 Kings 1)
- They will be able to stop the rain—Elijah (1 Kings 17:1)

- They can turn water into blood—Moses (Exodus 7:19–21)
- They can bring plague on the earth—Moses (Exodus 8,9,10,11)

They will minister in the temple at Jerusalem where they will preach against the Antichrist, and they will preach salvation to the unbelievers on the earth. They will be hated and feared because of their message from God, but no one will be able to keep them from completing their assignment. They will have been given a time limit of three and a half years; at the end of that time, they will have completed their ministry, and God will remove His protection from them. This is when the Antichrist will seize the opportunity to kill them. He is the only one who has this authority. Once he has killed them, he will be worshiped even more because of this great exhibition of his strength. The people will be so happy that the Antichrist has killed the two witnesses; they will make that day a holiday. They will start celebrating, even going as far as to exchange gifts with one another. All of this will take place in Jerusalem, the city God calls Sodom, and Egypt.

- Sodom: Because of their pride and indulgence
- Egypt: Because of their idolatry, persecution, and enslavement to sin

After the two witnesses are killed, their bodies will lie in the streets of Jerusalem for three days. The Antichrist will want the entire world to see that the witnesses are dead. He will also want everyone to know that he was the only one who could kill them. The Antichrist will then tell everyone that he is god. He will tell them that he is the one who should be worshiped, not the God of the two witnesses. At the end of three and a half days, God will put life back into the two witnesses. They will stand in the same spot where the Antichrist had left them for dead. Now the world will see that God has raised them from the dead just as he had done with His Son.

Then God will tell the two witnesses to come to heaven, and as they rise up into heaven, there will be an earthquake—not a worldwide earthquake. This earthquake will be felt only in Jerusalem where one-tenth of the temple will be destroyed and seven thousand people will be killed. Then the seventh angel will blow his trumpet to announce the beginning of the seven bowl judgments. These bowl judgments will come quickly, one right after the other. When the seventh trumpet is blown, the twenty-four elders will fall on their faces and worship God. They will know that the end is near, and that the Lord is taking back what is rightfully His.

TWELVE

As John was looking upward into the sky, a great sign appeared in heaven. It was the appearance of a woman wearing the sun, with the moon under her feet. She was wearing a crown of twelve stars, which is a symbol that would remind the Israelites of Gods covenant relationship with them.

- Women: represents Israel, the wife of God (Isaiah 54:5–6; Jeremiah 3:6–8; Genesis 37:9)
- Sun: represents glory, dignity, and the exalted status of Israel
- Moon: represents God's covenant with Israel—new moons were associated with worship (1 Corinthians 23:31; 2 Chronicles 2:4,8–13)
- Stars: represent the twelve tribes of Israel

The woman/Israel is pregnant and appears to be in labor. This is in reference to how Israel had suffered for centuries waiting for the Messiah to come. Here in verse 3, as John continued to look into the sky, he wrote about a second sign appearing. It was a red dragon, which is a representation of Satan. The red dragon had seven heads with crowns on them; he also had ten horns on his head. At this point, it seems that John take's us back in time before Satan was kicked out of heaven.

- Dragon: Satan
- Red: blood shed
- Seven heads: past kingdoms (Daniel 7:7, 20–21, 24): Egypt, Assyria, Babylon, Medo-Persia, Greece, Rome, and one future kingdom (Antichrist)
- Ten horns: future kingdoms that come from the one world government that will go to war against Jesus at the battle of Armageddon (Revelation 19:19)

In verses 3 and 4, we see the red dragon/Satan taking one-third of the stars/angels from heaven (Isaiah 14:12). This relates to when he was kicked out the first time, presumed to be before we inhabited the earth. In the next few paragraphs, it seems that John went back and forth in time in his description of Satan waiting to devour Israel's child. In verse 5, at the birth of Christ, Satan uses King Herod to kill all of the male children two years and younger in an effort to kill Jesus, the Messiah (Matthew 2:13–18; Luke 4:28–29).

Remember also that Satan knew that Jesus would come through the nation of Israel. That is why Satan used Pharaoh to kill the male children as described in the book of Exodus. Also, in the book of Esther, it is recorded that Haman tried to exterminate all of the Jews in the empire; this was also an attempt by Satan to completely destroy Israel.

And let us not forget Hitler, who was assumed to be under the influence of Satan in his effort to kill all Jews. The entire nation of Israel has always been under attack by Satan, and still is today. In verse 5, the child who was born (Jesus) was caught up to God (crucified and went to heaven).

Now John takes us into the future during the time of the Great Tribulation. In verse 6, we see that the woman (Israel) has to run and hide. Israel had to run and hide before, in AD 66 (Luke 21: 20–24), and then again during the middle of the Great Tribulation (Matthew 24:15–21; Daniel 12:1).

Some of the people will run and hide, and some will stay and fight. The place where they will hide in the wilderness will have been prepared for them by God. That place is thought to be the rock city of Petra or Bazrah in Saudi Arabia (Matthew 24:15–21; Daniel 12:1).

Also, if we look in the book of Daniel, we will see that the cities around Petra will not be destroyed by the Antichrist when he attacks the Holy City (Daniel 11:41). In verse 7, we ascend back into heaven where a war has begun between Michael the archangel and Satan.

Michael is the angel who is assigned to protect Israel. What a coincidence that Michael and Satan will start fighting when Israel has to flee for safety. Of course, Satan will lose again and will be cast out of heaven again, but this time he will be kicked out permanently. The first time Satan was thrown out of heaven, he still had the authority to go back and forth from heaven to earth as the accuser of the brethren (Job 1:6–7; 2:1–2). Satan will not be able to accuse us before God anymore because he will have lost his authority and access to heaven. Satan will been cast down to earth, never to return to heaven anymore. He will know his days are limited. A woe is given to the earth in verse 12 because Satan has lost his access to heaven and is going to take out his aggression on the people of the earth. When he is condemned to earth, he will direct his anger specifically toward Israel, but Gods protection will be greater than Satan's anger against her. As the people of Israel are escaping to the rock city of Petra for safety and shelter, the serpent/Satan will pour water like a river out of his mouth (verse 15). This water coming out of the mouth of Satan is a symbol of a large, fast-moving army. This army will try to stop the Israelites from trying to escape. Satan's army will be unsuccessful in stopping the Israelites because of Gods protection over them. So when Satan cannot harm them, he will turn his anger on the people who have refused to flee from Jerusalem. These are the ones who have given their lives to Christ during the Tribulation; they refused to take the mark of the beast.

Satan knew from the beginning when he deceived Adam and Eve that his time was limited. In the book of Genesis, we are told that a child would be born who would destroy Satan (Genesis 3:15). Satan knew that Jesus was the child who was prophesied in the Old Testament, and he was determined to destroy Him. This is why Satan has always tried to destroy Israel and the people associated with the birth of Jesus. Because of the prophet's messages of the imminent arrival of the king, everyone knew the Messiah was to come through the messianic linage of Adam. Satan wanted to preserve his time on earth and stay as long as he could, so he tried everything to prevent this child from being born. Satan was not able stop the birth of Jesus, so he tried to kill Him, and he thought he had killed Him when Jesus was crucified.

THIRTEEN

In Revelation 12:3, a description of the dragon is given: he has seven heads with seven crowns, and ten horns. In Revelation 13:1, the beast is described as having seven heads and ten horns with crowns on them.

The Bible is not specifically clear on the different descriptions, so this is what I think it means from some of my studies: The seven crowns on the seven heads in chapter 12 represent the six past kingdoms of the world—Egypt, Assyria, Babylon, Medo-Persia, Greece, and Rome. The seventh horn represents the Antichrist, a future kingdom (Revelation 17:10).

When John wrote this book of Revelation, five of the kingdoms had already been defeated: Egypt, Assyria, Babylon, Greece, and Medo-Persia. One was still in power, which was Rome. The seventh kingdom was yet to come, which will be influenced by the Antichrist. The crowns had moved from the six heads (past kingdoms) to the ten horns (future kingdoms). The ten horns represent the future kingdoms or nations that will be under the spiritual influence of Satan. We will read in coming chapters about how ten kingdoms will come to power, and Satan will kill three of their rulers. So, John takes us from the past kingdoms that were influenced by Satan to the future kingdoms that will be influenced by him. These ten kingdoms will be the ones that fight against Jesus at the battle of Armageddon. As we begin chapter 13, we are told that the dragon is standing on the sand of the seashore, and the beast is coming up out of the sea. The beast that John saw looked like a leopard with feet like a bear's and a mouth like a lion's. Then the dragon gave the beast his power, authority, and his throne.

- Dragon: Satan
- Sand of the sea: the nations that will be controlled by Satan
- Beast: the Antichrist
- Sea: humanity; the Gentile nation, unbelievers
- Lion: representative of fierceness
- Leopard: representative of speed
- Bear: representative of strength and stability

Whenever we see the word *beast* in the Bible, it does not represent an animal-like creature; rather, it represents a person who is influenced by a satanic spirit that controls him or her.

The nations that will rise up and defend the Antichrist will have the same spiritual influence controlling them.

These are the same spiritual forces that controlled the Egyptians, Babylonians, Greeks, and the Romans, who were seeking to control the world. The Medo-Persian kingdom was not used by Satan. God used them to free the Israelites from the Babylonians. It was predicted by Daniel in the book of Daniel that King Cyrus would come to power and free the Israelites from the Babylonians. It was in the form of prophecy 150 years before King Cyrus became king. He is the one who allowed them to return to Jerusalem to rebuild the temple (Isaiah 44–45; 2 Chronicles 36:22–23; Ezra 1:4–11).

One of the heads that John saw on the beast had a fatal wound that had been miraculously healed, and people of the whole earth were amazed. This head belonged to the Antichrist; this was his fake death and resurrection. The people will be fascinated when he appears to rise from the dead, and they will worship him. The world will follow the Antichrist and worship the dragon. In some translations of the Bible, the head that was wounded and healed is a nation that has been destroyed but will rise up again. In this scenario we can use Babylon, Rome, or Germany (Hitler) as examples. I am not referring to the actual form of government, but to the spiritual force that operated through these kingdoms and countries. This spiritual influence is still with us today. When the Bible says that the dragon gave them his power and authority, it refers to his spiritual influence. Nazi Germany is thought to have been under the same spiritual influence as the Roman Empire. Adolph Hitler was thought to be under the influence of Satan himself, and that is why the killing of the Jews was so important to him. Little is spoken about his obsession for finding the relics of the Bible; he spent millions of dollars trying to find the Ark of the Covenant and the Holy Grail. He thought they would give him the power of God. The Romans hated the Jews as well; they desecrated and destroyed the temple in Jerusalem around AD 68. The Babylonians enslaved the entire nation of Israel for seventy years.

I know that this type of spiritual influence is hard to believe, but the one thing you have to remember is that spirits do not die. They are eternal spiritual creatures; they live forever until they are thrown into the lake of fire. This is why, when we come under trials and tribulations, it is a spiritual influence that is trying to discourage, confuse, weaken, and possibly destroy us. We are attacked by the same spiritual influence over and over until we overcome it by our faith and the Word of God. We can use the Word of God along with our faith to defeat any spiritual influence that is coming against us

(Ephesians 6:11–18). That's why it is so important to know the Word of God for ourselves and learn to apply it to our circumstances. Verse 5 says that the beast is given permission to act; this permission comes directly from God.

How do we know this? Because he is given a time limit and permission. Why would Satan give himself a time limit to destroy humanity? He wants to kill as many of us as he can. We have to understand that Satan is a created being under the authority of God, just as we are. He will also be given the authority to speak blasphemy against God and to start killing the followers of Christ. Blasphemy is seeking to take the name of God for oneself.

Verse 8 is a little controversial, and this is what I mean: some would say that this verse implies that God chose all Christians before the creation of the earth; if God had not chosen you before the foundation of the earth, you cannot be saved. In other words, you don't have a choice (Deuteronomy 30:19; John 3:1–36).

God has always given us a choice; it's called free will. We must remember that John was writing about the times during the Great Tribulation. All who will live on the earth at that time are non-believers, and they will worship the Antichrist. Some will give their lives to Christ during the Tribulation, but the Antichrist will kill them. We, the church, are already in heaven. Our names are written in the Book of Life. In verse 11, John wrote about seeing a second beast rising up out of the earth. It had two little horns like a lamb, but it spoke like a dragon. This second beast—the false prophet—came from the land and will have the same power and authority as the first beast, the Antichrist. He will persuade the people on earth to worship the first beast, the Antichrist, who will perform great signs and wonders.

The second beast, the false prophet, will create a statue of the first beast, the Antichrist, for humanity to worship. This statue or idol will have the ability to speak. This is not the first statue or idol that has been built for people to worship. King Nebuchadnezzar of Babylon built a statue ninety feet tall; the entire kingdom was commanded to bow to it and worship it (Daniel 3).

Looking around today, we see idol statues all around us. There are statues of the Mormon angel Moroni in three states—Utah, California, and Washington DC. They range in height from twelve feet to twenty feet. In Brazil there is a statue of Jesus that is 125 feet tall. There are countless statues of Jesus, the Virgin Mary, and various saints in Catholic churches around the world.

Yes, these statues are built for idol worship. The second commandment says "thou shalt not make any graven image." Catholics bow down and pray to images of Mary. That is idolatry. Another point is that no one knows what Jesus looks like, so how can anyone make an image of Him? Do you have a picture of Jesus in your home?

Those who do not worship the idol of the Antichrist will be put to death. If that is not enough, the Antichrist will require all people to take marks on their foreheads or right hands. Without this mark, they will not be able to buy food or get the necessities of life. This is a way to force everyone to accept the idolatry of Satan.

During the time of the Roman Empire, a mark of this sort was normal for the identification of slaves, soldiers, and some religious cults. Satan will use his symbol in the same way the Romans used theirs—to recognize true followers. The number of the beast is 666. Six in the Hebrew language is the number of imperfect human being.

Satan will be the most powerful being on earth at that time, but he will still only be an imperfect being. The beast from the land, will be the final false prophet (Revelation 16:13, 19:20, 20:10).

The Antichrist will primarily be a political or military leader. The false prophet will be a religious leader; politics and religion will come together as a one-world religion that worships the Antichrist. A second beast will come from out of the earth; it will be a demon spirit coming from the abyss—the underworld, the realm of rebellious spirits and fallen angels, hell. The spirit will inhabit a person, a respected religious leader probably from Israel. This second beast/false prophet will have two little horns; this will show that he is subservient to the first beast, the Antichrist, who is described as having ten horns.

"Like a lamb" is a description of the false prophet imitating the true Lamb of God. This false prophet will appear to be gentle and attractive, but his mission will be the same as that of Satan and the Antichrist—to steal, kill, and destroy. He will perform signs and wonders. The miracles will be real, the signs will be real, but it will all be a deception to get humanity to follow the beast, otherwise known as Satan.

FOURTEEN

In chapter 14 of Revelation, we move forward into the future as we see Jesus on Mount Zion in Jerusalem with the 144,000 witnesses who were ministering on earth (Revelation 7:4). These witnesses will be taken up into heaven; they are described as standing around the throne. They will be singing a song that has been prepared specifically for them, and they will be the only ones who can sing it. This song is referred to as a song coming from the heart of someone who has been redeemed or delivered, a joyful song. These people will have walked the earth controlled by the Antichrist without defiling themselves. They will be blameless and loyal to the Father and to the Son. In verse 6, John wrote about seeing an angel flying through the air telling everyone that they still have time to repent. We are taught that humankind is to spread the gospel throughout the earth, and then the end will come (Matthew 24:14).

Here we see that it is an angel who will spread the gospel to every tongue and to every nation. God is about to pour out His final judgement on humanity as soon as the angel is finished proclaiming the gospel to every nation. A second angel following after the first will announce that Babylon has fallen. Babylon is a representation of the worldwide political, economic, and religious systems (Revelation

17 and 18). It is the same spiritual influence that controlled Babylon of the Old Testament and the Roman Empire of the New Testament. This event will happen in the midway point, three and a half years into the Tribulation. A third angel will appear and announce that anyone who has taken the mark of the beast will receive the wrath of God and will be tormented in hell for all of eternity. When the third angel appears, the Antichrist will have revealed himself to the world. The Babylonian religious system will have been destroyed, and the Antichrist will not need the church to hide behind anymore. He will proclaim that he is the messiah and that he should be worshiped.

The Antichrist will be in full view of the world for all to see; there will be no false religious system anymore. This is why the angel will say that anyone who takes the mark of Satan will receive the wrath of God. Those who have given their lives to Christ during the Tribulation will be encouraged to wait patiently, to obey God, and to not worship the beast. After all of the warnings of the wrath of God, it will now be time for the harvest to begin. Verse 14 is the beginning of the first harvest in the earth. John saw one like the son of man sitting on a white cloud (Revelation 1:13; Daniel 7:13–14). He will be wearing a golden crown and holding a sickle in His hand. He will swing His sickle over the earth, and it will be reaped. To reap is to gather the harvest. Jesus will gather the non-believers first, the ones who took the mark of the beast; they will be judged.

The next verse tells us that the second harvest will be directed at the nation of Israel, the vine of the earth (Psalm 80:8; Isaiah 5:1–7; Jeremiah 2:21, 6:9). This harvest will be a gathering of those who are in Israel who have been denying that Jesus is the Son of God. This harvest will then be put into a wine press called the wine press of the wrath of God. I see this harvest as judgment because the angel doing the reaping has power over fire, and fire is a symbol of judgment. The wine press is used to crush the grapes; it is also a sign of judgement.

FIFTEEN

In the previous chapter we see Gods mercy in action. He will send angels to tell everyone on the earth to repent, worship Him, and be saved from the wrath of God. In chapter 15 of Revelation, we see a different picture emerging. God will withdraw His troops from the battle. The 144,000 will surround the throne of God waiting to enter into heaven. Remember that, in chapter 14, we are shown the witnesses in Jerusalem on Mount Zion with Jesus. They will know that the time has come for the wrath of God to be poured out on all of the nations and mankind. They will know that the prophecies of God were about to be finished, and they will begin to sing a new song—a song of joy, a song of victory, a song of praise and worship to God that only they can sing. John looked into the sky and saw seven angels appear; these angel's are the ones who will carry out Gods final mission of wrath. The seven angels will be assigned to pour out the seven bowls of judgment on mankind and the earth.

The Bible calls the bowl judgments plague judgements. These bowls will hold plagues, and they will come one right after the other. The judgements in the bowls will increase in intensity and strength as we are quickly coming to the end of the Tribulation. As John continued to look into the heavens, he saw what he called a sea of glass mixed with fire. There were a number of people standing on the glass; these people are the ones who were killed during the Great Tribulation because of their belief in God and their refusal to worship the beast. These are the ones who listened to the angel in chapter 14 that was flying through the sky calling for the earth to repent. They did not worship the beast; they were singing the song of Moses, which is a song of deliverance from their enemies. This is the song that the Israelites sang after crossing the Red Sea and seeing the Egyptian army defeated.

They were also singing the song of the Lamb, a song of deliverance from sin by God, through Jesus Christ. These songs are made up of Old Testament quotes and testify to the righteousness of Gods judgments.

The next thing that was revealed to John was the opening of the Holy of Holies in the heavenly tabernacle. Another name for it is the temple of the tabernacle of testimony. This is the location where the Ark of the Covenant was kept when the tabernacle was in Jerusalem. The seven angels that John saw in the first verse will leave the presence of God, the Holy of Holies dressed in linen with golden sashes across their chests and around their waists. One of the creatures that sat around the throne of God will give the seven angels seven bowls containing the wrath of God. Each bowl will be shaped much like a saucer. They were used in the worship service in the tabernacle. Their flat shallowness shows that the judgments will be poured out quickly rather than slowly. Then the temple will be filled with smoke, and no one will be able to enter until the seven plagues have been poured out on the earth. Smoke filling the temple is a sign of the presence of God (Exodus 19, 16–18, 40:34–35; 1 Kings 8:10–11; Isaiah 6:4; Leviticus 9:23).

SIXTEEN

To compare the first judgments to the bowl judgments is to compare firecrackers to nuclear bombs. The bowl judgments are poured out one after the other with no break or interruption. John heard a voice coming from the temple that told the angels to pour out their bowls.

The first bowl judgment will be poured out on the earth. It will affect mankind in the form of boils on the skin (Exodus 9:9–11; Job 2:7; Luke 16:21). A boil is an infection of the hair follicle, a painful swollen area on the skin resulting in pus and dead tissue. This judgment will affect only those who have taken the mark of the beast. The second bowl will be poured out on the oceans. They will all turn to blood. This will not be like the second trumpet judgment when part of the seas turned to a blood-like liquid. This time, the substance will be thick, coagulated, like the blood that would accumulate around a human body that has been dead for a long time. When the oceans turn to blood, all of the vegetation that produces oxygen will die. When all of the oxygen in the ocean is gone, the creatures in the ocean will die. Can you imagine what the smell of coagulated blood along with dead plants and animals will be like? Remember, this will be happening over the entire earth!

The third bowl judgment will be poured out on the freshwater streams and lakes; their waters also will become like blood. When the third trumpet sounded (Revelation 11:6), one-third of the earth's fresh water supply turned poisonous. With this judgement, most, if not all, of the drinking water on the earth will be contaminated. No one will be able to use it. "For they poured out the blood of saints and prophets and you have given them blood to drink" (Revelation 11:6).

In Revelation 11:7 we read, "True and righteous are your judgments." How can the God of love be true and righteous by pouring out these bowl judgements on humanity? The question should be, what took God so long to judge the unsaved? We have to remember that God is a just God; He did not judge us or give us what we deserved sooner because of His mercy and His grace. I do not think that we realize that God has been merciful to mankind for thousands of years. He could have said, "That's it! I'm done with these humans!" And he could have destroyed the earth and everything in it. He did not do that because He loves us that much (2 Peter 3:7–15).

In Revelation 11:8, we read that the fourth bowl will be poured out on the sun, and mankind will be tortured with intense heat. The sun, a sustainer of life, will become the killer of humanity. The heat from the sun will be so hot that all of the ice and snow of the North and South Poles will melt (Amos 8:8, 9:5–6). Still, people will not repent and give God the glory that He deserves. Remember that the previous chapters recorded that the sun will become dim. Whatever is in this bowl definitely turns the heat up.

The fifth bowl will be poured out onto the Antichrist and the city in which he lives, which has come to be known as his kingdom. The city and all of its inhabitants will be thrown into total darkness. This will not be darkness as we know it today; rather, it will be a darkness that can be felt on the skin. Along with the darkness will come an indescribable pain that is so intense that the people will chew their tongues off. Have you ever bitten your tongue? Can you imagine what kind of pain you would have to be in to make you chew it entirely off?

- You will have boils on your skin.
- There will be no fresh water to drink.
- The sun will be burning you.
- You will be in indescribable pain.
- You will be able to feel the darkness all around you.

This is the part that I do not understand. The people still will not recognize God and repent of their sins! How stubborn and blind do you have to be to not want all of this to *stop*?

It is amazing how much punishment these people will go through and still not accept God. This is the time to pause and think of your friends and family members who are not saved and who will be going through all this pain and suffering. Is that why God has you reading this book? So that you can tell them what you have learned about Jesus and the coming judgments?

The sixth bowl will be poured out on the earth. The Euphrates River will dry up. What is the significance of this? Those who fight in the battle of Armageddon—the armies of the Antichrist -vs- Jesus, will have to cross this river to enter the battleground in the valley of Megiddo, also known as the valley of Jezreel (Daniel 11:40–45; Joel 3:9–11; Psalm 2:1–6).

Note: Napoleon called the valley of Megiddo the perfect battlefield. Here are some other battles fought at this location:

- Britain vs Turkey — after this battle the land became Israel 1948
- Joshua vs King Megiddo — Joshua 12:21
- Gideon vs Midianites — Judges 7

- Saul vs the Philistines — 1 Samuel 28–31
- Deborah and Barak vs Canaan — Judges 5:19

At this time, we are getting extremely close to the return of Jesus who will come with His army ready to go to war with the Antichrist. We are almost at the three-and-a-half-year point of the Great Tribulation, and the Euphrates River is the crossing point for the army of the Antichrist. The Euphrates River is the eastern boundary of the Promised Land. These kings and their armies will be able to reach Palestine by walking across the dry riverbed.

Isaiah 11:15–16 relates that God will supernaturally dry up the river to specifically draw these kings into this location for battle. In verse 13 states that John saw three unclean spirits come out of the mouth of the dragon, the beast, and the false prophet. Here we see a description of the unholy trinity, another attempt by Satan to be like God and the Holy Trinity. These three demon spirits will deceive the leaders of this world into sending their armies across the Euphrates River to fight against Jesus and His army. These demons are described as looking like frogs. Frogs are unclean animals according to Old Testament dietary law. Persian mythology viewed them as plague-inducing creatures. These demons will trick the leaders of these armies into invading Palestine and going to war with Jesus.

Even with the pain of their sores, the heat, the drought, and darkness, the people will still cross the river to do the biding of the Antichrist (Psalm 2:2; Joel 3:2–4).

Verse 15 is thrown in for the believers who converted to Christianity during the Great Tribulation. The message is this: "I know you see the armies of the Antichrist coming, and it is a great army, but do not be afraid, I am coming soon" (1 Corinthians 15:58; Galatians 6:9).

The seventh bowl will be poured out with a voice from the throne in heaven saying, "It is finished." The wrath of God on humanity will be finished; the Great Tribulation will have ended. The greatest earthquake known to history will destroy all of the mountains on the earth. All of the islands will disappear. Great quantities of hail stones will fall from the sky. Jerusalem will be split into three separate parts (Zechariah 14:1–8).

In Luke 21:25–28, we read that there are still people who have not repented. Instead, they will blame God and curse Him for what is happening.

Babylon, the capital city of the Antichrist, will receive a special outpouring of the wrath of God as prophesied in the book of Isaiah (Isaiah 13:6–13). Chapters 17 and 18 detail the destruction of spiritual Babylon, which will already have fallen.

SEVENTEEN

Chapter 17 of Revelation begins with the Great Tribulation and ends about three and a half years into the Great Tribulation. It will end after or during the sounding of the sixth trumpet in chapter 9. So that there is no confusion, some of the events that happen in the book of Revelation happened at the same time or one right after the other.

Chapter 17 begins with the judgement of the great whore who sits on the waters (Revelation 17:1). This person may be female or male; the reason the word *whore* is used is that it represents the spirit of idolatry and the abandonment of the religious principles that we are familiar with today.

This false religious spirit was the beginning of a worldwide false religion, a new-world-order religion that excludes the truth about God, His work, and His people. This spirit began in Babylon around 300 BC when King Nimrod disobeyed God and settled in the land known as Babel. We are living in the beginning of a resurgence of this false religion today; after the Great Tribulation, it will take over completely.

In Genesis 9:1, we read that God told Noah and his descendants to "be fruitful, multiply and fill the earth." In this same chapter, verse

7, God repeated His commandment: "populate the earth, abundantly populate it." Nimrod and those with him decided that they wanted to settle in the land known as Babylon. Nimrod was made king or ruler of Babylon because he was a great hunter, a mighty one on the earth (Genesis 9:1, 11; Genesis 10:8–10). How did Nimrod become a king, and why is he not mentioned in the book of Kings? And what was the source of his power that made him a great hunter?

Disclaimer: The following information is not in the Bible; it is in a manuscript that was found in Israel known as the Ancient Book of Jasher. This manuscript is referenced in Joshua 10:13, 2 Samuel 1:18, and 2 Timothy 3:8.

When Adam and Eve sinned, God killed an animal and used the skin of the animal to cover them. I know you were taught that He covered them with fig leaves, but God did not do that. The killing of this animal was the first blood animal sacrifice. The animal skins that God used to cover them were passed down from generation to generation beginning with Seth, Adam's third son. The skins then went to Methuselah, Noah's grandfather, then to Lamech, Noah's father, then to Noah. Noah's son Cush stole the animal skins and gave them to his son Nimrod. Because of the sacrifice that God had made to cover the sins of man, His anointing was still on the animal skins. And this is where Nimrod received his power, but he used this power for evil. He was a mighty hunter before the Lord (Genesis 10: 8–10).

For more information about this, I recommend reading the book *The Two Babylons* by Alexander Hislop (1853) and the *Ancient Book of Jasher* by Ken Johnson.

The spirit of pride entered King Nimrod, and he deserted the teachings of his father, Cush, the son of Ham, the son of Noah, and disobeyed God by settling in the land of Babel. Remember that God had told them to keep going and to populate the land; they disobeyed God and built a city called Babylon.

Because of the power he possessed, he and his wife wanted to be worshiped. His wife, Semiramis, especially wanted this. She led him to build the tower of Babel. Then he led his people into the worship of idols and formed a paganistic religious system.

King Nimrod's pride got the best of him, and he attempted to build a tower to reach to heaven. "For we will be gods" is what he said. God had to intervene and change the language of the people so they could not understand each other; therefore, they could not continue building the tower (Genesis 11:1–9).

Of course, Satan was the influence behind the whole idea, and in this chapter, we see the final rise and fall of this pagan religion. This false religious spirit has been around for many years as you have read, and it has influenced many nations and empires.

A lot of churches today operate under this same false religious influence, but chapter 17 of Revelation tells us where it all will end. This worldwide false religion will ignite like a wildfire at the beginning of the Tribulation, but it will last for only three and a half years. In the first verse, we are told that this spirit has a female influence, and we are told that *she* is sitting on many waters.

Sitting means that she has authority over what she is sitting on—the many nations. When water is mentioned in the Bible, it is usually associated with Gentiles, so we believe she has authority over Gentile nations. The second verse relates that the people have committed themselves to this false world religion. In the third verse, we read that John was taken to the wilderness by an angel, and he was shown this woman riding on a scarlet beast. She has power over the beast and the kings of the earth (military leaders) until the middle of the Great Tribulation. She is dressed in the finest clothes and the most expensive jewelry (Revelation 3:14–17). All of her fancy clothes and jewelry represent luxury, splendor, and the royalty of this world; they are used to distract the people. They see all of the things that she has, and they think that by worshiping this false religion, they can have them as well. The scarlet beast that she is riding is the Antichrist. Her riding on the beast is a symbol of his support for her. Satan is behind all of this, waiting for his chance to be worshiped as a god. The beast has seven heads and ten horns, with the names of blasphemy written on his heads. A blasphemy is anyone or anything that claims to be a god. She is drunk with the blood of saints. These saints are the Christians who will be killed during the Tribulation. These are the ones who will not take the mark of the beast or worship this pagan religion (v.9–10).

- Seven heads: Past kingdoms (Daniel 7:7, 20–21, 24): Egypt, Assyria, Babylon,
- Medo-Persian, Greece, Rome, with one to come.
- Ten horns: Future kingdoms, that come from the one world government (v.12)

When John wrote this, Rome was the dominating empire in the world the "one that is." Five other kingdom's had fallen: Egypt, Assyria, Babylon, Medo-Persia, and Greece. The empire to come is the Antichrist. All of these kingdoms were inhabited by the same Satanic spirit of world domination that ruled Babylon, Rome, and Germany. Verse 11 speaks of an eighth power or spirit. The eighth one is Satan; he is the one who is using all of this to get what he has always wanted—to be worshiped as god. He wants to use this false religious system to unify the world kingdoms and gain control for himself. He will destroy this false religious system, through the Antichrist, and the ten world leaders, verse 16 says that they will burn her and eat her. Then the ten world leaders will give their authority and power to Satan (v.12–13).

In actuality they will be carrying out Gods will (v.17). These same ten world leaders are the ones who will bring their armies against Jesus at the battle of Armageddon (Revelation 16:14–16).

As a reminder, this chapter begins around the time when the Great Tribulation will begin, and it ends around the time of the sixth trumpet in chapter 9. So, while the bowls are being poured out, Satan will proclaim he is god and therefore does not need the religious system anymore. Now all forms of religion will be eliminated from the earth. Satan will require the people on earth to take his mark, the mark of the beast.

(a) John wrote that the angel offered to explain to him the mystery of the woman and of the beast. (b) (Both a king and a kingdom are referred to by this term.) The beast that John saw was the *spirit* that had controlled the Roman Empire in the past. It broke up and no longer exists as a world empire today. This same spirit will ascend out of the bottomless pit (the same spirit that controlled the Roman Empire). It will reappear and go to perdition (eternal punishment). It will be utterly and finally destroyed.

(c) This statement could also refer to one of the kingdoms that was destroyed and is revived. (Rome not the actual city of Rome but the spirit that guided them).

After his resurrection, the Antichrist will become possessed by a great demon from the abyss. The phrase "go to destruction" refers to the lake of fire, the place of the Antichrist's destruction.

(a) *Believers Bible Commentary* (Nashville TN: Thomas Nelson Publishing, 1995)

(b) *New American Standard Bible*, comments section verse 8 Page 1986 (Nashville TN: Thomas Nelson Publishing, 2006)

(c) *New American Standard Bible*, comments section verse 3 Page 1986 (Nashville TN: Thomas Nelson Publishing, 2006)

EIGHTEEN

Chapter 18 of Revelation is about the destruction of the political, commercial, and economical system of Babylon. The one-world political system will fail as will the one-world financial system. This also will also bring an end to the commercial system of Babylon. In chapter 17, we read that the Antichrist will declare himself god and that everyone must worship him or die.

The government will no longer be functioning; martial law will be proclaimed. Only the nations that have strong, stable militaries will be in control, and the Antichrist will control the nations that control the military.

Sounds like a great plot for a movie, except this is real. There will be no money, no formal government, no resources. What do you think will happen to the people who have survived to this point? What is life going to be like? We can only imagine. According to scripture, there will be ten nations that will join the Antichrist to control the earth—yes, the entire earth. The Jews who have survived will realize that they have made a terrible mistake in claiming the Antichrist as god, and they will renounce him. When this happens, he will turn on them and will destroy what is left of Jerusalem and anything that will remind the people of the one true God. The Jews will flee to the Rock City of Petra in Jordan where an angel of the Lord will protect them. The temple in Jerusalem will be desecrated, and the Antichrist will stand in the temple and once again declare that he is god. He will make a sacrifice to himself on the altar of God. Then he will destroy the city of Jerusalem. Babylon will be destroyed—the same commercial, political, and economical, system that operates in the earth today, yes today. Look around at the world systems that we operate in today. The financial systems make the rich richer. The political systems support the rich. Laws are passed to help them keep their wealth. This commercial system controls the cost of everything. That's why, when you get a raise in pay, the cost of products and goods are raised as well. We are always trying to catch up, always in debt, and all of this is by design.

In verse 1, we read that an angel will announce that Babylon has fallen, and the system will no longer operate the way it was designed to. The world will cry out for Babylon. Why? Because of their love for her? No, because of their loss of the luxury and pleasure that she brought to them. As you can see, this affects the entire world trade system (v.12–19).

Heaven will rejoice because of her final destruction. God will have avenged the death of His prophets and the people whom she has destroyed because of their faith. This will mark the beginning of the end of the Great Tribulation. In verse 1, we see that the angel will come to earth surrounded by a great light. Remember that, at this point in time, the earth is in darkness (Revelation 16:10).

So, when the angel shows up, everybody will see him, and everyone will hear him. He will tell the people that Babylon has fallen, that she has been destroyed. Once religious Babylon falls as described in chapter 17, the people will worship their false gods and materialistic things even more. Political and industrial leaders were consumed with this worldwide Babylonian system. The fourth verse is very interesting. It explains that God will tell His people to "come out of her." Who is He talking to? All of the Christians are in heaven. So, this means that some of those who did not make it into heaven will call Jesus their Lord and savior and become born again. That is why the call is made to come out of the Babylonian system and to repent.

NINETEEN

In chapters 17 and 18 of Revelation, we have seen the destruction of the spirit of the Babylonian political and finical system. Was it destroyed by God? Perhaps it was, but physically it was destroyed by Satan. Revelation 17:16 tells us that the ten kings will eat her flesh and burn her with fire. "Her" refers to the spirit of Babylon.

We read in Revelation 17:17 that God will put it in their hearts to kill her, so in a sense she will be destroyed by God. Revelation 18:8 explains that she will be burned with fire because of the judgement of God against her. Remember that the events recorded in chapters 17 and 18 have already happened. Take a look back to Revelation 14:8, which says "fallen is Babylon the great." Chapters 17 and 18 give us an historical understanding of what has already happened. In Revelation 19:1, we read, "After these things." What does "things" relate to? We have to go back to the things that were described in chapter 16—the bowl judgements. If we read chapters 14 through 16 and then skip to chapter 19, we may have a better understanding of the order of events.

Now, as we begin to study chapter 18, we read about a loud shout of "Hallelujah!" coming from heaven. This shout will be the rejoicing heard in heaven because the spirit of Babylon has been judged and has been defeated. In the New Testament, the word *hallelujah* appears only four times, each one in this chapter. I know, I said the same thing: "What?" But if you do your research, you will find this to be a true statement (Revelation 19:1; 19:3; 19:4; 19:6). The reason for celebration is that God has avenged the blood of His servants. A second shout of hallelujah will be heard when the members of the heaven see the smoke coming from the burning city of Babylon.

The twenty-four elders and the four living creatures will all fall down and worship God by shouting "Hallelujah!" A voice will come from heaven saying, "Give praise to our God." Then John heard a loud sound like thunder saying "Hallelujah, the Lord our God reigns."

His judgements are true and righteous, this is the reason for the shout of Hallelujah.

Hallelujah means "praise the Lord.: *Alleluia* is the Greek word for praise. *Halal* is the Hebrew word for "praise." *Jah* means "Jehovah" or "Lord."

Then it will be time for the invitation to the marriage supper of the Lamb and His Bride, which is the church. Throughout the entire Bible, we are told that the church is the bride of Christ. We are told that those who have been forgiven of their sins will one day participate in a wedding and a feast, or communion, with Him.

As we look at the eighth verse, we see that the bride is dressed in white linen, an expression of being righteous or of being clean: "The righteous acts of the saint's" These righteous acts are the things that we have done that show or prove that God lives inside of us. This is not the righteousness that God puts in us when we are born again; rather, it is the righteous acts we have done since we have become Christians. The friends of the bridegroom are the saints who have died during the Old Testament era before the day of Pentecost (Acts 2).

The guests will also include the Tribulation saints, those who became Christians during the Great Tribulation period. The church is the bride presented in heaven to Jesus Christ. Then we will come to earth for the marriage supper. This is a celebration that will take place during the Millennium Kingdom period, the one-thousand-year reign of Christ. After the wedding and before we come for this supper, Jesus will return with us as His army. This is when Jesus will destroy the army of Satan at the battle of Armageddon. In verse 17, we read that an angel will call the birds to come to "the great supper of God," which is not to be confused with the marriage supper. This supper is to clean up all the dead bodies after the battle of Armageddon. After this war, Jesus will cast the Antichrist and the false prophet into the lake of fire.

Note: The spirit of prophecy is the testimony that Jesus is the only way to get to heaven, that He is the son of God, and that He is the final sacrifice for our sins. So if people come to you and say "I have a prophetic word for you" or "I prophecy that you will do something," if it is not about Jesus, tell them to keep that prophetic word for themselves (Revelation 19:10).

Here's a question I think about: In Revelation 19:4, the four living creatures are called beasts. Throughout the book of Revelation, Satan is called the beast. Could Satan have possibly been, at one time, one of the living creatures or beasts that surrounded the throne of God? As far as I know, the King James Version of the Bible is the only Bible that calls the living creatures beast.

TWENTY

Satan will be bound for one thousand years, and we, the born-again believers, will reign with Christ for one thousand years. The rebellion of the fallen angels will end. The sinners will be cast out or sent to the lake of fire for eternity. Again, it sounds like a plot for a great movie, but it is not.

In the first verse, we read that an angel will come down from heaven with the keys to the Abyss and a chain for restraining Satan. In the next verse, we read that the angel who came down from heaven will grab the devil by the throat, tie him up, and throw him into the Abyss, a prison where demons and fallen angels will be held until they are cast into the lake of fire. (Okay it did not say he grabbed him by the throat; that's just how I want to see it!)

Not all of the fallen angels and demons will be bound. Some will be allowed to roam around heaven and earth (Revelation 9:1–12). Ultimately, however, all fallen angels and demons will be cast into the lake of fire (Revelation 20:10).

After Satan is bound, he will be locked away for one thousand years. This period is called the Millennium Kingdom period. *Millennium* is Latin for one thousand. There are three different views of what the Millennium Kingdom will be.

1. Premillennialism: Jesus will return to earth before this thousand-year period. This would be the fulfillment of prophecy

2. (2 Samuel 7:12–16; Psalm 2; Isaiah 11:6–12, 24:23; Hosea 3:4–5; Joel 3:9–21; Amos 9:8–15).

3. Postmillennialism: Jesus will reign on earth through the Christians on earth.

4. A-millennialism: We are living in the thousand-year period now.

In Revelation 20:3, we read that Satan will be released from the pit at the end of this thousand-year period, but only for a short period of time. In verses 7–9, we are told that Satan will be released from the pit into the earth. Remember that once this thousand year period has ended, the Millennium Kingdom will have ended.

In Revelation 20:8, we read that he will deceive the nations and gather them together for war! If you are like me, you have always believed that, once Satan has been put in the pit, evil will be completely wiped out. And then there is the question of where did the sinners come from? How can sin enter the earth when it is perfect?

Satan will be released so that God can make a permanent end to sin before establishing the new heaven and the new earth. There will be those who will give their lives to Christ during the Great Tribulation. When Jesus returns, they will be accepted into the Millennial Kingdom in their human bodies; therefore, they will still have the ability to reproduce, and they will have children during the millennial period. Their offspring will be given a chance to accept Jesus or reject Him as their savior. Some will not accept Jesus and will rebel against God, just as they do today. They will join with Satan in a final battle that will completely eradicate sin. They will come from all four corners of the earth. Their number will be like the sand at the sea. When Satan and this army come against the Lord, fire will come down from heaven and kill them all. After this, all of the graves will be opened and all of the people who have died will stand before the Lord. The Book of Life will be opened, and all those whose names are not written in it will be cast into the lake of fire. In Revelation 20:4, we see thrones, and those who sit on them are the judges. Then the Christians who were killed during the Great Tribulation will be raised from the dead. However, everyone who has died will not be resurrected at that time; some unbelievers will remain in their graves. When they are raised from their graves to stand before God at the great white throne of judgment. This will be the end of the millennial period; this is known as the second resurrection.

Those who sat on the throne are the church, you, and me (Revelation 2:26–27; Revelation 3:21; 1 Corinthians 6:2–3).

There will be two resurrections:

1. The first resurrection is the resurrection of life, also known as the resurrection of the righteous. It is divided into five parts (1 Corinthians 15:20–23):
   a) Jesus, (1 Corinthians 15:23) already finished (fulfilled)
   b) Church-age saints, from the time of Pentecost to the beginning of the Great Tribulation (1 Thessalonians 4:16,17)
   c) Two witnesses (Revelation 11:11–12)
   d) Old Testament saints (Isaiah 26:19; Daniel 12:2)
   e) Christians who died during the Tribulation (Revelation 20:4)

2. The second resurrection is the resurrection of judgment (John 5:28–29;
3. Acts 24:15). This is the final judgment, the great white throne of judgement.

If we are part of the first resurrection, we will not have to worry about the second death. Yes, there are two deaths as well. The first death is the death of the body, the flesh, a physical death. The second death is an eternal separation from God. After the second death, people will be cast into the lake of fire to be tormented for eternity.

So, at this point in time, we see Jesus sitting on a throne ready to judge. Heaven and earth as we know them will be gone. In Revelation 20:11, we read that the heaven and earth will flee; they will not exist anymore. All men and women will exist in spirit only; there will be no more fleshly human bodies (2 Peter 3:10–13).

Sinners will be standing in front of the throne—the great white throne of judgement—to be judged. The sinners will not be the only ones standing before a throne; those who believe in Jesus Christ will also be judged at the Bema Seat of Christ (Romans 14:10–12; 2 Corinthians 5:10; 1 Corinthians 9:4–27).

We, as Christians, will judged based on what we have done—our deeds—from the time we became born again until the time of this judgement. Our thoughts will be judged (Luke 8:17; Romans 2:16). Our words will be judged (Matthew 12:37). Our actions will be judged (Matthew 16:27). Our deeds will be compared to God's standards (Matthew 5:48; 1 Peter 1:15–16).

At the Bema Seat of Christ, we will receive our crowns (2 Timothy 2:5; 4:8; James 1:12; 1 Peter 5:4; Revelation 2:10).

Revelation 20:12 tells us that there will be three books opened: two for the unbelievers, and one for believers. People whose names are not in the Book of Life will be cast into the lake of fire; they will experience death and hell. This is the second death. I have to point out to you that there will be Christians condemned to the lake of fire as well, but when I say Christian, I mean those who claim to be Christians but are not.

Not everyone who says to Me, Lord, Lord; will enter the kingdom of heaven, but he who does the will of My Father who is in heaven will enter. *Many* will say to Me on that day, Lord, Lord, did we not prophesy in Your name, and in Your name cast out demons, and in Your name perform many miracles? 23 And then I will declare to them, *I never knew you*, depart from me you who practice lawlessness. (Matthew 7:21–23, emphasis mine)

Also see Matthew 7:13–29; Luke 6:46; and James 1:22–25; 2:26.

This is the ending of the Sermon on the Mount where Jesus describes two gates, two ways, two groups of people, two kinds of trees, two kinds of fruit, and two groups of judgment. So, what will happen when everyone has been judged? Will all things be made new? Or will things just return to what God had intended for them to be before sin entered the earth?

TWENTY-ONE

As we begin looking at chapter 21 of the book of Revelation, it is difficult to imagine all of the things that have been recorded in the first twenty chapters. It has been revealed to us what will happen to those who are left behind. We have also been told what will happen to the earth, the sun, the moon, and the stars. But the most exciting part is in chapter 4, we learn that the church will be taken out of the earth and received into heaven.

There will also be some people who will give their hearts to the Lord during the time of the Great Tribulation. They will not see a physical death; rather, they will enter the Millennium Kingdom in their human form (Jeremiah 1:5).

I know you probably have not thought about it in this way, but you must study the book of Revelation for yourself. Pray and ask God to give you understanding. The book of Revelation in the past has been looked upon as predicting the future. It is taught that you have to have a special anointing or training to understand or teach from this book. This is totally not true. All you have to do is read it and ask God to open your mind and expand your understanding of what you have read. The book of Revelation is not a mystical book of ancient origin; it's God's warning to us of what will happen if our names are not written in the Book of Life.

The word of God says, "My people are destroyed because of *their* lack of knowledge" (Hosea 4:6).

If you do not understand the scriptures, you will fall or fail (Hosea 4:14). This does not mean that you are going to hell; it just means that you will fail or have a difficult time when the trials and tribulations come your way. The trials and tribulations are normal; we must go through them. But they do not have to become a reality in our lives. If you do not know that the Word of God teaches you how to handle these trials and tribulations, you will have to endure difficult times.

The Bible is a road map. Follow it and you will reach your destination. That destination is the new heaven and the new earth; it is where we will worship God and spend eternity with Him. The capital city of the world will be the New Jerusalem where God will make His home.

Verse 1 tells us that the entire universe will be destroyed and then recreated (2 Peter 3:10–13; Psalm 102:25–26; Isaiah 65:17, 66:22; Luke 23:33; Hebrews 1:10–12). In verse 2, John writes that he saw the New Jerusalem coming down from heaven; that means that it already existed. The New Jerusalem is where God will make His home, His tabernacle (Leviticus 26:11–12; Deuteronomy 12:5).

There will be no more tears, no more pain, no death. All of these things will be taken away. Old value systems will change, priorities will change, our beliefs and plans will all change. This new city will be made of everything that we now know as valuable or being priceless: gold, pearls, and precious gemstones. But the one thing that this city will not have is a temple, a physical place to worship God. There will be no temple in the New Jerusalem because God will be living with us. He will be the temple. There will be no sun or moon;

the city will shine with the glory of God, and His glory will give light to the entire world. The angel who spoke to John, as we read in verse 15, gave him the measurements of the city: 1,500 square miles, a perfect cube.

Just to give you an idea of what the size of the new city will be, think of the area from the Canadian border to the Gulf of Mexico, from the Atlantic Ocean to the state of Colorado. The new city will have a wall around it. This wall will be a representation of God's protection around us. The wall will be two hundred-sixteen feet high, and there will be three gates on each side of each the wall. Each gate will represent one of the tribes of Israel, and above each gate will be the name of each tribe. There will be twelve foundations representing the twelve apostles who laid the foundation of the church.

Note: The number twelve represents the establishment of a government or administration. This number is used twenty times in the book of Revelation and seven times in chapter 21 alone. God is setting up His government.

TWENTY-TWO

In verse 1 John wrote, "then he showed me." He refers to the same angel mentioned in Revelation 21:9. He is also one of the seven angels who poured out one of the seven bowl plagues. What he showed John was a river coming from God's throne; this river is called the river of life. This river will not be like a river we would recognize; remember there will be no hydrological cycle, meaning there will be no rain. The clouds will have been removed, so there will be no system to produce water. We read in chapter 6 that the system will be destroyed when the angel opens the sixth seal. The river of life is a symbol of the continuous flow of eternal life from God to us who live in heaven (Revelation 7:17; John 4:13–14, 7:37–38). On both sides of the river, trees will be growing, but there will be only one variety of tree—the tree of life. This tree will no longer be forbidden as it was in the Garden of Eden; it will grow twelve different kinds of fruit, one type for each month. The leaves on the trees will be for healing. The word *therapeutic* comes from the Greek word that is translated as "healing." So, I guess we will need some sort of therapy, mental or physical. The curse of sin, at this point, will have been removed; God will be in control, and we will serve Him. We will finally get to see

His face. His name will be written on our foreheads, and His glory will light the world. In verse 6, we read that the angel will confirm that everything that he has shown John is from God. In verse 7, we read blessed is he that keeps the sayings of the prophecy of this book.

We are to pay attention to what is in the book of Revelation, and when we do, we will receive blessings. What type of blessings? I don't know, but if God will bless me for reading, hearing, and keeping His word, count me in. The angel told John do not seal the words of this book, meaning that he was to make the information available to everyone.

When prophecy is given, it is given to us for direction. God is giving us a warning that we are out of His will. He is warning us of what the future will hold according to His mercy, grace, and wrath. Those that reject the prophecy will continue in their evil ways, and eventually will face the wrath of God. Those who accept the prophecy will practice righteousness and will receive the blessings of the Lord. In verse 13, Jesus verifies who He is, and in verse 16, Jesus tells us that He is the one who sent the angel to John. In verse 18, we are given another warning: anyone who adds anything to what is written in the book of Revelation will suffer all of the plagues described in the book.

If anyone misinterprets, falsifies, or alters the meaning of what is written, his or her name will be removed from the tree of life (22:2). He or she will also be restricted from coming into the Holy City, the New Jerusalem. How many millions of dollars have been generated from books predicting what will happen to mankind according to this book?

CLOSING

Why study the book of Revelation—the last book of the Bible? If we know the end, or the future in this case, we can make better decisions in our lives today. When I first began studying the book of Revelation, the first thing that stood out to me was that I would receive a blessing for reading or hearing this particular book. No one had ever told me that. Then I remembered that I had read this book many times, and I had not realized, or recognized, what was said in the first chapter: "*Blessed* is he that reads and hears the words of this prophecy, and *keeps* or *understands* those things that are written." In these last days, God will reveal Himself in His Word. In other words, He will open our eyes to the knowledge He is releasing. He will reveal things that were once hidden. Why hidden? First, because it was not time for them to be revealed, and second, because we would not have understood what He was telling us.

His Word cannot be revealed until we reach the point of getting the Word of God into our hearts. When we first became born-again believers, we read the Bible but we do not understand it. We read it because that was the thing to do. Now as we have grown in Christ, we read the Bible for understanding and guidance. Our hearts have changed. We have a desire, and we have a need for the Word of God because it brings peace to our lives. The Word of God gives us an understanding of the things that are happening around us. When we understand the Word of God, we understand who God is; we understand His mercy and His grace. We understand how much God really loves us when we learn of the spiritual love He has for us. It is the kind of love that exceeds our physical three-dimensional realm of understanding. This spiritual love takes us to a different level of understanding of what love is through His eyes and through His heart. Once I started to concentrate on the Word of God rather than just reading it for the sake of reading it, I received the wisdom, knowledge, and understanding of who God is and why He sent His Son to us.

Bibliography

Arnold, Bill T. and Bryan E. Beyer. *Encountering the Old Testament: A Christian Survey.* Grand Rapids, Michigan: Baker Publishing Group, 2015.

Lumpkin, Joseph B. *The Books of Enoch.* Alabama: Fifth Estate, 2009.

MacArthur, John. *The MacArthur Study Bible.* La Habra, California: Nelson Publishing Company, 2006.

Macdonald, William. *Believers Bible Commentary.* Nashville Tennessee: Thomas Nelson Publishing, 1995.

Swete, Henry Barclay. *The Apocalypse of St. John*, third edition. London: Macmillan Publishers, 1922

Wiersbe, Warren W. *Be Distinct.* Colorado Springs, Colorado: David C. Cook, 2010.

Printed in the United States
by Baker & Taylor Publisher Services